izza with Kale, Pancetta & Chile Oil (page 45)

the pizza cookbook

DEVELOPED BY

WILLIAMS
SONOMA

TEST KITCHEN

Photographs **Erin Scott**

weldon**owen**

CONTENTS

Making Pizza at Home 7

Pizza Equipment 8

Pizza Dough Primer 10

Recipes 13

Index 61

Serrano Ham & Grilled Pineapple Pizza
with Smoked Mozzarella (page 52)

Pesto Pizza with Summer Squash,
Sweet Corn & Pecorino (page 35)

Making Pizza at Home

Authentic homemade pizza is more achievable now than ever before. Cooks benefit from both a greater knowledge of classic pizza styles and how to duplicate them, as well as from sophisticated equipment designed for the home kitchen and backyard. A ceramic pizza stone in a hot conventional oven is still the most popular way to bake pizza, but aficionados regularly adapt recipes to work equally well in outdoor grills and brick ovens as well as in contemporary countertop pizza ovens.

Most modern pizza makers strive for a lightly charred, evenly blistered, and chewy crust—the result of both a terrific dough recipe and the high heat used to bake it. However, the characteristics of a top-rate pizza dough are really a matter of personal preference, so we offer several different recipes—from a dense Sicilian crust best suited for a pan pizza to cornmeal, gluten-free, and cheese-stuffed crusts, plus the thin flatbread-style Roman crust and the chewy, slow-rising Neapolitan crust.

Sauces and toppings are secondary but essential components. They're the easiest way to change up the flavor profile of any pizza—especially when you choose the best local and seasonal ingredients. For light, summery flavors, we incorporate fresh toppings such as tomatoes, zucchini, peaches, figs, and fresh arugula. White pizza is also a favorite, so we often make Potato, Bacon & Rosemary Pizza (page 26) with a white sauce of garlic and Parmesan, and a pizza of shaved asparagus (page 22) with melted leeks and a creamy base of melted burrata. Pizza with Kale, Pancetta & Chile Oil (page 45) is robust enough to stand up to a thick Sicilian crust, as is the Salsiccia Pizza with Padrón Peppers (page 56) and a Spanish-inspired pie (page 40) topped with romesco sauce, chorizo sausage, and plenty of shaved Manchego cheese, though any crust will work with these zesty blends. The combinations of pizza toppings are endless, so you'll have lots of opportunities to experiment.

Pizza Equipment

When it comes to pizza making, the essential tools are really quite basic. The recipes in this book were tested using a wooden pizza peel and a ceramic pizza stone in a hot conventional oven. Both are excellent choices for making pizza at home. However, there are many other methods from which to choose. These recipes can be easily adapted for baking in a hot grill (either directly on the grill rack or on a cast-iron pizza pan or ceramic pizza stone), in an outdoor pizza oven, or in any of the countertop pizza ovens now available. (See right for a few of our favorite countertop options.) Timing and temperature will vary with each device, so consult the manufacturer's instructions for assistance in making any recipe alterations.

ROCCBOX PIZZA OVEN

Roccbox is the world's first portable outdoor stone-floor pizza oven. From Britain's leading manufacturer of commercial pizza ovens, the Roccbox bakes authentic Neapolitan pizza in under 90 seconds. The countertop oven achieves temperatures of up to 930°F using a wood burner for authenticity and a gas burner for convenience, expertly heating the pizza stone inside to replicate the stone-cooked flavor of professional pizza ovens. A unique safe-touch silicone jacket protects users and kitchen countertops from the intense heat. The oven is light enough for one person to carry and includes a strap for easy transport.

BREVILLE PIZZAIOLO

The Pizzaiolo is Breville's first countertop oven developed exclusively for baking pizza. Reaching temperatures up to 750°F, the Pizzaiolo features a unique dual heat-source oven technology that radiates heat from two circular panels of a high-performing electric heating coil system—one below the ceramic stone pizza deck and one above the pizza while it bakes. Set the top and bottom heat according to the desired pizza style, using lower temperatures for frozen and thick-crust pan pizzas, mid-range heat for New York–style pizzas, and high heat for the lightly blistered and charred crusts characteristic of traditional wood-fired Neapolitan pizza.

Countertop pizza ovens are compact, high-performing alternatives to built-in backyard ovens and capable of achieving similarly high temperatures.

Pizza Dough Primer

MIXING & KNEADING

Preparing pizza dough from scratch is really quite easy. The recipes in this book use an electric stand mixer for mixing and kneading, but that's not the only method for making top-notch dough. Yeast dough can be prepared by hand, of course, and also with a food processor. Dough mixed by any of these methods will not vary perceptibly, so choose the technique you prefer.

To mix and knead dough in a stand mixer, combine the yeast, sugar, and water in the mixer bowl and let stand until foamy, about 5 minutes. Add the flour and salt. Using the paddle attachment, mix on medium-low speed just until combined. Let stand for 10 minutes, then switch to the dough hook and knead on low speed (slowly adding the oil, if called for in the recipe) until the dough comes together in a ball, pulls cleanly from the sides of the bowl, and springs back when gently pressed with a fingertip, about 10 minutes.

To mix and knead dough by hand, combine the yeast, sugar, and water in a large bowl and let stand until foamy, about 5 minutes. Add the oil, if called for in the recipe, and the salt. Gradually stir in as much of the flour as possible until the dough is too stiff to mix. Dump the remaining flour out onto a work surface and place the dough on top. Knead the dough, incorporating as much of the flour as needed to prevent sticking, until the dough is smooth and springs back when gently pressed with a fingertip, about 10 minutes.

To mix and knead dough in a food processor, combine the yeast, sugar, flour, and salt in the processor bowl and pulse to mix. With the processor running, slowly add the water (and the oil, if called for in the recipe) until the dough comes together in a rough mass. Let it rest in the processor for 5–10 minutes, then process for 30 seconds to fully develop the protein and make the dough resilient.

RISING

After mixing and kneading, yeast doughs need to rise at room temperature for about 1 hour, but can also rise in the refrigerator overnight. Rising time will have some effect on the final texture—a slow rise will yield a thicker, chewier Neapolitan-style crust, while a fast rise and a bit of olive oil will produce a thinner, crispier Roman-style crust.

Place the kneaded dough in an oiled bowl (or leave in the mixer bowl if kneaded with a stand mixer). Cover the bowl with plastic wrap and let the dough rise until about doubled in bulk, about 1 hour at room temperature or at least 8 hours or up to 48 hours in the refrigerator, punching down the dough after the first 24 hours. Bring refrigerated dough to room temperature for about 1 hour before shaping.

SHAPING

Shape the pizza dough according to personal preference, your choice of toppings, and the dimensions of your pizza stone and/or cooking appliance.

Turn the dough out onto a lightly floured work surface and press flat to release any air. Divide it into the desired number of pizzas. Roll out the dough with a rolling pin or press with your fingertips from the center to the edges. Handle the dough minimally to avoid activating the gluten, which will make it difficult to shape. To relax the gluten, cover the dough lightly with plastic wrap and let stand for 10 minutes, then try again. Slip a floured pizza peel under the rolled-out dough, add the toppings, and bake as directed.

BAKING

Pizzas can bake at temperatures ranging from 425°F in a conventional oven to 750°F or higher in large outdoor pizza ovens and in small ones designed for indoor use (see page 8). Lower temperatures yield crusts that rise slowly and are a bit denser; higher temperatures produce crusts that rise quickly, resulting in larger pockets of air and a chewier texture.

Preheat a pizza stone in a conventional oven, grill, or pizza oven. Place the pizza peel holding the topped pizza over the hot stone. Quickly pull the peel from beneath the pizza in one swift movement. Bake the pizza until the crust is golden brown, 7–8 minutes at 425°F or 2–3 minutes at 750°F. Check the pizza during baking, using the peel to move it if needed for even browning. When the pizza is ready, use the peel to transfer it to a cutting board. Cut the pizza into slices and serve.

Pizza Doughs

Regular Crust Slow Dough

¾ teaspoon active dry yeast
¾ teaspoon sugar
⅔ cup lukewarm water (about 115°F)
1½ cups bread flour
¾ teaspoon kosher salt
Olive oil, for the bowl

In the bowl of a stand mixer, stir together the yeast, sugar, and water. Let stand until bubbles form on top, about 5 minutes. Fit the mixer with the paddle attachment. Add the flour and salt and beat on medium-low speed just until combined, about 30 seconds. Let stand for 10 minutes. Switch to the dough hook and knead on low speed until the dough comes together into a ball and pulls away from the sides of the bowl, about 10 minutes.

Transfer the dough to a lightly oiled bowl, cover the bowl with plastic wrap, and refrigerate for at least 8 hours or up to 3 days. Remove the dough from the refrigerator and let stand, covered, at room temperature for 1 hour. Divide the dough in half, roll out to the desired size, then top and bake.

Makes two 6-oz dough rounds

Thin Crust Fast Dough

1½ teaspoons active dry yeast
¾ teaspoon sugar
¾ cup lukewarm water (about 115°F)
1½ cups bread flour
1 teaspoon kosher salt
2 teaspoons olive oil

In the bowl of a stand mixer, stir together the yeast, sugar, and water. Let stand until bubbles form on top, about 5 minutes. Fit the mixer with the paddle attachment. Add the flour and salt and beat on low speed until combined. Switch to the dough hook. Slowly drizzle in the oil and knead until the dough comes together into a ball and pulls away from the sides of the bowl, about 5 minutes.

Remove the bowl from the mixer and cover the bowl with plastic wrap. Let rise at room temperature until the dough is doubled in size, about 1 hour.

Divide the dough in half, roll out to the desired size, and cover loosely with plastic wrap or a kitchen towel. Let stand at room temperature for 20 minutes before topping and baking.

Makes two 6-oz dough rounds

VARIATION

Cornmeal Pizza Dough

Replace the 1½ cups bread flour with 1 cup bread flour and ¾ cup cornmeal.

Sicilian Crust Dough

1½ tablespoons active dry yeast

1 teaspoon sugar

1½ cups lukewarm water (about 115°F)

4 cups all-purpose flour

1 tablespoon kosher salt

1 cup cool water

½ cup olive oil, plus more for greasing

In the bowl of a stand mixer, stir together the yeast, sugar, and lukewarm water, then stir in ½ cup of the flour. Cover the bowl with plastic wrap and let stand for 15 minutes. Fit the mixer with the paddle attachment. Add the remaining 3½ cups flour, the salt, the cool water, and ¼ cup of the oil and beat on low speed until the dough just comes together, about 1 minute. Switch to the dough hook and knead on medium-low speed until the dough is smooth, about 10 minutes; the dough will be very wet. Remove the bowl from the mixer and cover the bowl with plastic wrap. Let rise in a warm spot until the dough is doubled in size, about 1 hour.

Preheat the oven to 450°F.

Grease a rimmed baking sheet. Transfer the dough to the prepared pan and stretch it evenly to the sides and corners. Using your fingers, make indentations in the top of the dough, then drizzle with the remaining ¼ cup oil. Top and bake as directed.

Makes one 14-oz dough round

Gluten-Free Pizza Dough

Olive oil, for greasing

3 cups gluten-free flour (we recommend Cup 4 Cup), plus more for dusting

1 tablespoon kosher salt

1 teaspoon baking soda

2 large eggs

2 tablespoons olive oil

⅔ cup water

Generously grease a baking sheet with olive oil. Set aside.

In a large bowl, mix the flour, salt, and baking soda. In a small bowl, stir together the eggs, oil, and water. Make a well in the flour mixture and pour in the egg mixture. Mix until the dough comes together, then use your hand to knead the dough against the side of the bowl a few times to form a ball. Divide the mixture in half. Work with one piece of dough at a time. Place one dough half on a clean kitchen towel or piece of parchment paper dusted with flour. Flatten the dough with your hands, then use a rolling pin dusted generously with flour to roll out the dough to the desired size. Use the towel or parchment to flip the dough onto the prepared baking sheet. Top and bake as directed. Repeat to use the remaining dough half for another pizza.

Makes two 6-oz dough rounds

NOTE: This pizza dough is best enjoyed fresh out of the oven, when it is still hot and crispy.

Use a rolling pin with discretion when rolling out pizza dough, since too much handling will activate the gluten in the dough, making it difficult to stretch and shape.

Tomato Sauce (at right)

Sauces

Tomato Sauce

2 tablespoons olive oil

2 cloves garlic, minced

½ cup dry white wine

1 bay leaf

1 can (28 oz) crushed tomatoes

1 tablespoon tomato paste

2 teaspoons sugar

1 teaspoon dried oregano

Kosher salt and freshly ground pepper

½ cup fresh basil leaves, finely chopped (optional)

In a large sauté pan over medium heat, warm the oil. Add the garlic and cook, stirring occasionally, until fragrant, about 1 minute. Add the wine and bay leaf and bring to a simmer, then cook, stirring occasionally, until reduced by half, about 5 minutes. Add the tomatoes, tomato paste, sugar, oregano, and a pinch each of salt and pepper. Simmer, stirring occasionally, until the sauce thickens and the flavors deepen, about 20 minutes. Remove from the heat and adjust the seasoning with salt and pepper. Remove and discard the bay leaf. Stir in the basil, if using. Let cool. Use right away, or transfer to an airtight container and refrigerate for up to 1 week.

Makes about 2⅔ cups

Romesco Sauce

2 jarred roasted red peppers (about ⅓ cup)

2 cloves garlic, smashed

½ cup almonds, toasted

2 tablespoons tomato paste

2 tablespoons sherry vinegar

1 teaspoon smoked paprika

Pinch of cayenne pepper

½ cup olive oil

Kosher salt

In a food processor, combine the peppers, garlic, almonds, tomato paste, vinegar, paprika, and cayenne and process until finely chopped. With the processor running, add the oil in a steady stream and process until almost smooth. Stop the processor and scrape down the sides of the bowl, then process until smooth, about 10 seconds longer. Season to taste with salt. Use right away, or transfer to an airtight container and refrigerate for up to 1 week.

Makes about 1½ cups

White Sauce

3 tablespoons unsalted butter
3 tablespoons all-purpose flour
1¼ cups whole milk
1 clove garlic, grated
½ cup (2 oz) grated Parmesan cheese
Kosher salt and freshly ground pepper

In a small saucepan over medium-low heat, melt the butter. Add the flour and cook, whisking constantly to prevent lumps from forming, until a thick paste forms, 3–4 minutes. While continuing to whisk, slowly add the milk. Cook, stirring often, until the mixture is thick enough to coat the back of a spoon, about 4 minutes. Add the garlic and cheese and cook, stirring often, until the sauce reaches the consistency of a thick gravy, about 4 minutes longer. Reduce the heat to low if the sauce starts to scorch. Season to taste with salt and pepper. Let cool. Use right away, or transfer to an airtight container and refrigerate for up to 3 days.

Makes about 1 cup

Basil Pesto

1 cup tightly packed fresh basil leaves
¼ cup (1 oz) grated Parmesan cheese
¼ cup pine nuts, toasted
1 clove garlic
⅓ cup olive oil
Kosher salt

In a food processor, combine the basil, cheese, pine nuts, and garlic and pulse until finely chopped. With the processor running, add the oil in a steady stream and process until combined. Season to taste with salt. Use right away, or transfer to an airtight container and refrigerate for up to 2 weeks or freeze for up to 2 months.

Makes ½ cup

VARIATION
Arugula Pesto

Make the Basil Pesto as directed, but substitute the 1 cup basil with 1 cup arugula.

Basil Pesto
(at left)

Tomato Sauce
(page 17)

Romesco Sauce
(page 17)

White Sauce
(at left)

Fresh herbs, seasonal vegetables
and fruits, and an inspired collection
of sauces, salumi, and cheeses
are primary among the abundant
choices of pizza toppings.

Toppings

Once you have a good pizza dough at the ready, your selection of toppings is essential to establishing the flavor profile of your pie. The old adage of the more, the better doesn't necessarily hold true here. In fact, you should resist the temptation to pile on the ingredients. A few carefully selected elements will ensure that each one shines. Cheese should also be used prudently, so that it doesn't overwhelm the mix. Employ simplicity for garnishes as well, such as a sprinkle of coarse salt to enhance the flavors, a drizzle of olive oil for an attractive sheen, a scattering of red pepper flakes for a touch of heat, or a small handful of torn herbs for a bright, fresh finish.

USE SEASONAL INGREDIENTS

Use the best-quality and freshest ingredients you can find, purchasing them from local growers or farmers' markets if possible. An inspired selection of fresh, in-season components will provide an easy harmony of ingredients and the greatest depth of flavor. Don't miss asparagus in spring, tomatoes in summer, squash in autumn, hardy greens in winter—the peak of each season's harvest will contribute the most flavor to any combination.

EXPLORE COMPLEMENTARY FLAVORS

When pairing ingredients in any dish, matching the intensity of flavors is a good rule of thumb. A spicy Italian sausage is an apt partner for bitter leaves of kale and a hearty tomato sauce. Rich, slow-cooked onions set the stage for the sharp taste of gorgonzola, salty prosciutto, and sweet, ripe figs. You can also mix ingredients according to their country of origin, such as chorizo and manchego, or their peak season, such as spring asparagus and leeks or summer corn and zucchini. Consider the elements that are natural companions on the plate, then couple them on your pie—even if they are ones not commonly used atop pizza. Shaved lemons, for example, are an unexpected but welcome partner to chunks of calamari, as is fresh tarragon to chopped clams, and squash blossoms to thinly sliced zucchini. Unconventional but naturally complementary ingredients can result in the most memorable pizzas, so use some imagination in addition to personal taste when deciding on possible topping combinations.

Pizza with Shaved Asparagus, Melted Leeks & Burrata

Burrata, the rich Italian cheese featuring an outer shell of mozzarella enveloping a filling of stracciatella and cream, makes an easy foundation for pizza. For a bright finish, grate a bit of lemon zest over the top before serving.

Place a pizza stone in the oven. Preheat the oven to 425°F.

In a bowl, toss together the asparagus and oil, and season with salt and pepper. Set aside.

In a frying pan over medium heat, melt the butter. Add the leeks and cook, stirring occasionally, until softened, about 10 minutes. Add the garlic and cook, stirring occasionally, until fragrant, about 1 minute. Season with salt and pepper. Let cool.

On a lightly floured surface, roll out the dough to a 12-inch round. Transfer the dough to a floured pizza peel. Tear the burrata into 1-inch pieces over the dough, distributing it evenly and leaving a 1-inch border uncovered. Arrange the leeks and asparagus on top and sprinkle with ¼ cup of the Parmesan.

Transfer the pizza to the preheated stone. Bake until the crust is crisp and golden brown, 7–8 minutes.

Using the pizza peel, transfer the pizza to a cutting board and sprinkle with the remaining ¼ cup Parmesan and a few grinds of pepper. Cut the pizza into slices and serve.

Serves 4

4 asparagus spears, trimmed and thinly shaved

2 teaspoons olive oil

Kosher salt and freshly ground pepper

4 tablespoons unsalted butter

6 oz leeks, white and pale green parts, halved lengthwise and cut crosswise into ¼-inch slices

1 clove garlic, grated

All-purpose flour, for dusting

1 ball (6 oz) Pizza Dough (pages 13–14)

½ lb burrata cheese, drained

½ cup (2 oz) grated Parmesan cheese

For the greatest ease in shaving the asparagus spears, use a serrated vegetable peeler designed for soft vegetables.

Quattro Staggioni Pizza

Literally "four seasons pizza," a pizza quattro stagioni features four different toppings, one on each of the four quadrants of the pie. Although they often vary, usually each ingredient represents one of the seasons. Here, artichokes denote spring, olives summer, mushrooms autumn, and ham winter.

Place a pizza stone in the oven. Preheat the oven to 425°F.

In a small bowl, toss together the mushrooms and oil, and season with salt and pepper.

On a lightly floured surface, roll out the dough to a 12-inch round. Transfer the dough to a floured pizza peel. Spread the romesco sauce evenly over the dough, leaving a 1-inch border uncovered. Arrange the toppings in separate quadrants of the pizza: the mushrooms on one quarter, the olives on another, the artichoke hearts on another, and the ham on the final quarter.

Transfer the pizza to the preheated stone. Bake until the crust is crisp and golden brown, 7–8 minutes.

Using the pizza peel, transfer the pizza to a cutting board and sprinkle with the cheese. Cut the pizza into slices and serve.

Serves 4

3 oz cremini mushrooms, sliced

1 tablespoon olive oil

Kosher salt and freshly ground pepper

All-purpose flour, for dusting

1 ball (6 oz) Pizza Dough (pages 13–14)

1/3 cup Romesco Sauce (page 17)

1/3 cup pitted black olives, halved

2/3 cup marinated artichoke hearts, quartered

2 oz thinly sliced serrano ham

2 tablespoons grated Parmesan cheese

Potato, Bacon & Rosemary Pizza

The marriage of potato and bacon with a white garlic sauce is a classic pairing of Alsace, France, while the rosemary roots the flavors in the Italian tradition. The light sauce and thin potato slices work especially well over a thin crust.

Place a pizza stone in the oven. Preheat the oven to 425°F.

In a small frying pan over medium heat, cook the bacon, stirring occasionally, until just cooked through, about 5 minutes. Transfer to a paper towel–lined plate and let cool, then cut into ¾-inch dice.

In a small bowl, stir together the white sauce and chopped rosemary. In another small bowl, toss the potato slices with the oil and a big pinch each of salt and pepper.

On a lightly floured surface, roll out the dough to a 14-inch oval. Transfer the dough to a floured pizza peel. Spread the rosemary–white sauce evenly over the dough, leaving a 1-inch border uncovered. Arrange the potato slices on top, followed by the bacon.

Transfer the pizza to the preheated stone. Bake until the crust is crisp and golden brown, 7–8 minutes.

Using the pizza peel, transfer the pizza to a cutting board and sprinkle with the rosemary leaves and a few grinds of pepper. Cut the pizza into slices and serve.

Serves 4

¼ lb sliced bacon

⅓ cup White Sauce (page 18)

1½ teaspoons chopped fresh rosemary, plus 1 tablespoon rosemary leaves

1 Yukon gold potato, very thinly sliced

1 tablespoon olive oil

Kosher salt and freshly ground pepper

All-purpose flour, for dusting

1 ball (6 oz) Pizza Dough (pages 13–14)

Use a mandoline or a very sharp knife to slice the potatoes as thinly as possible and ensure even cooking.

Pizza with Guanciale & Fried Sage Leaves

Guanciale is a robustly flavored cured meat made from pork jowl or cheeks. If you can't find guanciale, pancetta makes a fine substitute.

In a small frying pan over medium heat, cook the guanciale until crisp and cooked through, 7–10 minutes. Transfer to a paper towel–lined plate and set aside.

Place a pizza stone in the oven. Preheat the oven to 425°F.

On a lightly floured surface, roll out the dough to a 12-inch round. Transfer the dough to a floured pizza peel. Spread the white sauce evenly over the dough, leaving a 1-inch border uncovered. Arrange the guanciale on top, season with pepper, and sprinkle with 2 tablespoons of the cheese.

Transfer the pizza to the preheated stone. Bake until the crust is crisp and golden brown, 7–8 minutes.

Meanwhile, in a small sauté pan over medium heat, pour in canola oil to a depth of 1 inch and heat until shimmering. Add the sage leaves and cook until the bubbling slows, 1–2 minutes. Using a slotted spoon, transfer the sage leaves to the paper towel–lined plate and season with salt. (Discard the sage-infused oil or set aside for another use.)

Using the pizza peel, transfer the pizza to a cutting board, sprinkle with the remaining 2 tablespoons cheese, garnish with the fried sage leaves, and drizzle with the chili oil. Cut the pizza into slices and serve.

Serves 4

2 oz guanciale or pancetta, cut into ¼-inch pieces

All-purpose flour, for dusting

1 ball (6 oz) Pizza Dough (pages 13–14)

⅓ cup White Sauce (page 18)

Kosher salt and coarsely ground pepper

¼ cup (1 oz) grated Parmesan cheese

Canola oil, for frying

¼ cup fresh sage leaves

1 teaspoon chili oil

White Pizza with Fresh Clams & Tarragon

Littleneck clams steam in white wine, butter, and tarragon, then partner with a creamy garlic sauce in this elegant pizza. Garnish with extra tarragon.

In a saucepan over medium heat, warm the oil. Add the shallot and cook, stirring occasionally, until softened, about 3 minutes. Add the garlic and cook, stirring, for 1 minute. Add the clams and 3 of the tarragon sprigs and stir to coat. Add the wine and butter and stir until the butter melts, about 2 minutes. Reduce the heat to low, cover, and cook until the clams have opened, 10-12 minutes. Using a slotted spoon, transfer clams to a bowl. Discard the tarragon sprigs and any clams that did not open. Cook the sauce over medium-low heat, stirring often, until reduced by half, about 15 minutes.

Place a pizza stone in the oven. Preheat the oven to 425°F.

Meanwhile, remove half of the clams from their shells and coarsely chop the meat; reserve the remaining clams for topping the pizza. Stir the meat into the sauce and set aside.

Finely chop the leaves from the remaining tarragon sprig and stir into the white sauce. On a lightly floured surface, roll out the dough to a 12-inch round. Transfer the dough to a floured pizza peel. Spread the tarragon–white sauce evenly over the dough, leaving a 1-inch border uncovered. Spread the clam sauce evenly over the white sauce.

Transfer the pizza to the preheated stone. Bake until the crust is just golden, 5-6 minutes. Using the pizza peel, remove the pizza from the oven and top with the clam shells. Bake until the clams are just heated through, about 2 minutes longer.

Using the pizza peel, transfer the pizza to a cutting board. Cut the pizza into slices and serve with lemon wedges.

Serves 4

3 tablespoons olive oil

1 shallot, diced

5 cloves garlic, thinly sliced

1 lb littleneck clams, soaked in salted water for 30 minutes, then drained

4 fresh tarragon sprigs

½ cup dry white wine

2 tablespoons unsalted butter

Kosher salt and freshly ground pepper

½ cup White Sauce (page 18)

All-purpose flour, for dusting

1 ball (6 oz) Pizza Dough (pages 13–14)

Lemon wedges, for serving

Mozzarella & Grana Padano Pizza with Truffle Oil & Arugula

The beauty of this pizza lies in its simplicity and the quality of the ingredients. Grana padano is a hard, slow-ripened Italian cheese comparable to Parmesan. Its saltiness is tempered here with creamy mozzarella, slightly spicy arugula, and a touch of rich truffle oil.

Place a pizza stone in the oven. Preheat the oven to 425°F.

On a lightly floured surface, roll out the dough to a 12-inch round. Transfer the dough to a floured pizza peel. Sprinkle the mozzarella evenly over the dough, leaving a 1-inch border uncovered. Sprinkle with ¼ cup of the grana padano.

Transfer the pizza to the preheated stone. Bake until the crust is crisp and golden brown, 7–8 minutes.

Meanwhile, in a small bowl, toss together the arugula and olive oil, and season with salt and pepper.

Using the pizza peel, transfer the pizza to a cutting board, sprinkle with the remaining ¼ cup grana padano, drizzle with the truffle oil, and top with the arugula. Cut the pizza into slices and serve.

Serves 4

All-purpose flour, for dusting

1 ball (6 oz) Pizza Dough (pages 13–14)

½ lb fresh mozzarella cheese, torn into 1-inch pieces

2 oz (about ½ cup) grated grana padano or Parmesan cheese

2 cups arugula

1 tablespoon olive oil

Kosher salt and freshly ground pepper

2 tablespoons truffle oil

Sei Formaggi Pizza

Sei, the Italian word for "six," refers to the collection of cheeses that crowns this enticing pie, including Parmesan, feta, Asiago, Gorgonzola, and two types of mozzarella. Feel free to sub in your favorite Italian cheese varieties—pecorino, provolone, ricotta, and fontina are all good choices.

Place a pizza stone in the oven. Preheat the oven to 425°F.

On a lightly floured surface, roll out the dough to a 12-inch round. Transfer the dough to a floured pizza peel. Spread the tomato sauce evenly over the dough, leaving a 1-inch border uncovered. Sprinkle evenly with all of the cheeses except the Gorgonzola.

Transfer the pizza to the preheated stone. Bake until the crust is crisp and golden brown, 7–8 minutes.

Using the pizza peel, transfer the pizza to a cutting board. Sprinkle on the Gorgonzola and let stand for 1 minute. Cut the pizza into slices and serve.

Serves 4

All-purpose flour, for dusting

1 ball (6 oz) Pizza Dough (pages 13–14)

¼ cup Tomato Sauce (page 17)

2 oz fresh mozzarella cheese, diced

½ cup (2 oz) shredded mozzarella cheese

1 oz feta cheese, crumbled

2 tablespoons grated Parmesan cheese

2 tablespoons grated Asiago cheese

1 oz Gorgonzola cheese, crumbled

Pesto Pizza with Summer Squash, Sweet Corn & Pecorino

Make this summery pizza at the height of the season, when fresh corn, basil, and zucchini are plentiful and at their best. Finish the colorful pie with a little flaky sea salt for a pleasing crunch and, if you like, a few squash blossoms, available at farmers' markets during the summer months.

Place a pizza stone in the oven. Preheat the oven to 425°F.

On a lightly floured surface, roll out the dough to a 14-inch oval. Transfer the dough to a floured pizza peel. Spread the pesto evenly over the dough, leaving a 1-inch border uncovered. Arrange the zucchini and squash ribbons on top and season with salt and pepper. Sprinkle with the corn kernels and 2 tablespoons of the cheese.

Transfer the pizza to the preheated stone. Bake until the crust is crisp and golden brown, 7–8 minutes.

Using the pizza peel, transfer the pizza to a cutting board and sprinkle with the remaining 2 tablespoons cheese, the lemon zest, and flaky sea salt. Drizzle with oil and garnish with squash blossoms, if using. Cut the pizza into slices and serve.

Serves 4

All-purpose flour, for dusting

1 ball (6 oz) Pizza Dough (pages 13–14)

¼ cup Basil Pesto (page 18)

½ zucchini, thinly shaved lengthwise

½ yellow summer squash, thinly shaved lengthwise

Kosher salt and freshly ground pepper

⅓ cup fresh corn kernels

¼ cup (1 oz) grated pecorino cheese

2 teaspoons grated lemon zest

Flaky sea salt and olive oil, for garnish

Squash blossoms, for garnish (optional)

Heirloom Tomato Pizza Margherita

Good pizza Margherita recipes keep it simple, focusing on just a few high-quality ingredients. Use the best heirloom tomatoes you can find and include a mix of colors and sizes. Before placing the tomato slices on the dough, be sure to salt them, which draws out the juices, and then pat dry.

Place a pizza stone in the oven. Preheat the oven to 425°F.

Place the tomato slices in a single layer on a kitchen towel or paper towels. Season with salt and let stand for 10 minutes. Pat dry with the towels and season generously with pepper.

On a lightly floured surface, roll out the dough to a 12-inch round. Transfer the dough to a floured pizza peel. Spread the oil evenly over the dough, leaving a 1-inch border uncovered. Arrange the tomato slices on top and sprinkle with the mozzarella.

Transfer the pizza to the preheated stone. Bake until the crust is crisp and golden brown, 7–8 minutes.

Using the pizza peel, transfer the pizza to a cutting board and sprinkle with the Parmesan and basil. Cut the pizza into slices and serve.

Serves 4

12 oz heirloom tomatoes, cut into slices about ¼ inch thick

Kosher salt and freshly ground pepper

All-purpose flour, for dusting

1 ball (6 oz) Pizza Dough (pages 13–14)

1 tablespoon olive oil

3 oz fresh mozzarella cheese, torn into 1-inch pieces

½ cup (2 oz) grated Parmesan cheese

¼ cup torn fresh basil leaves

Artichoke & Anchovy Pizza

A little cayenne pepper and a healthy dose of red pepper flakes give basic tomato sauce a spicy new profile. The piquant sauce is balanced by bold Mediterranean toppings that hit all the right notes—marinated artichoke hearts, briny olives and capers, and salty anchovies and Parmesan.

Place a pizza stone in the oven. Preheat the oven to 425°F.

In a small bowl, stir together the tomato sauce, red pepper flakes, and cayenne.

On a lightly floured surface, roll out the dough to a 12-inch round. Transfer the dough to a floured pizza peel. Spread the spicy tomato sauce evenly over the dough, leaving a 1-inch border uncovered. Arrange the olives, artichokes, and anchovies on top. Sprinkle with the capers and 2 tablespoons of the cheese.

Transfer the pizza to the preheated stone. Bake until the crust is crisp and golden brown, 7–8 minutes.

Using the pizza peel, transfer the pizza to a cutting board and sprinkle with the remaining 2 tablespoons cheese. Cut the pizza into slices and serve.

Serves 4

⅓ cup Tomato Sauce (page 17)

½ teaspoon red pepper flakes

¼ teaspoon cayenne pepper

All-purpose flour, for dusting

1 ball (6 oz) Pizza Dough (pages 13–14)

¼ cup pitted Kalamata olives, halved

¼ cup marinated artichoke hearts, quartered

8 anchovy fillets in olive oil

2 tablespoons capers, chopped

¼ cup (1 oz) grated Parmesan cheese

Fig & Prosciutto Pizza with Caramelized Onions & Gorgonzola

The contrast of sweet and salty offset with the sharpness of Gorgonzola strikes a nice balance in this delicious recipe. Balsamic glaze drizzled over the top just before serving adds another layer of luscious tangy flavor.

In a frying pan over low heat, melt the butter. Add the onion and season with salt and pepper. Cook, stirring occasionally, until the onion is meltingly tender and rich brown in color, about 40 minutes; do not let it burn. Let cool.

Meanwhile, place a pizza stone in the oven and preheat the oven to 425°F.

On a lightly floured surface, roll out the dough to a 12-inch round. Transfer the dough to a floured pizza peel. Spread the fig jam evenly over the dough, leaving a 1-inch border uncovered. Sprinkle with the cheese and top with the caramelized onion.

Transfer the pizza to the preheated stone. Bake until the crust is firm but not crisp, about 5 minutes. Using the pizza peel, remove the pizza from the oven and top with the fig slices. Return to the oven and bake until the figs are slightly caramelized and the crust is crisp and golden brown, 2–3 minutes.

Using the pizza peel, transfer the pizza to a cutting board, drape the prosciutto over the pizza, and drizzle with the balsamic glaze. Cut the pizza into slices and serve.

Serves 4

3 tablespoons unsalted butter

1 small yellow onion, thinly sliced

Kosher salt and freshly ground pepper

All-purpose flour, for dusting

1 ball (6 oz) Pizza Dough (pages 13–14)

3 tablespoons fig jam

2 oz Gorgonzola cheese, crumbled

3 small figs, cut into $1/8$-inch slices

1 oz thinly sliced prosciutto

Balsamic glaze, for drizzling

Chorizo & Manchego Pizza with Oregano Oil

Incorporating many iconic ingredients of Spain, this dense pizza showcases zesty Spanish chorizo sausage, the aged sheep's milk cheese known as Manchego, and romesco sauce made with roasted red peppers and almonds. A drizzle of oregano-infused olive oil lends the finishing touch.

Place a pizza stone in the oven. Preheat the oven to 425°F.

To make the oregano oil, in a small bowl, stir together the oil and oregano, and season with salt and pepper.

On a lightly floured surface, roll out the dough to a 12-inch round. Transfer the dough to a floured pizza peel. Spread the romesco sauce evenly over the dough, leaving a 1-inch border uncovered. Sprinkle with the Manchego and mozzarella and arrange the chorizo in a single layer on top. Drizzle with the oregano oil.

Transfer the pizza to the preheated stone. Bake until the crust is crisp and golden brown, 7–8 minutes.

Using the pizza peel, transfer the pizza to a cutting board and sprinkle evenly with the oregano leaves. Cut the pizza into slices and serve.

Serves 4

½ cup Romesco Sauce (page 17)

FOR THE OREGANO OIL

2 tablespoons olive oil

2 teaspoons dried oregano

Kosher salt and freshly ground pepper

All-purpose flour, for dusting

1 ball (6 oz) Pizza Dough (pages 13–14)

¾ cup (3 oz) shaved Manchego cheese

¼ cup (1 oz) shredded mozzarella cheese

¼ lb cured Spanish chorizo, cut on the diagonal into ¼-inch slices

2 tablespoons fresh oregano leaves

Oregano oil imbues this simple pie with herbaceous flavor. Make extra oil for adding at the table, if you wish.

Sausage Pizza with Fennel & Ricotta

Fresh fennel becomes mellow and almost sweet when cooked—the ideal partner for mild Italian sausage. Cut each fennel wedge through the core to keep the layers intact during cooking. A blend of ricotta and mozzarella plus a last-minute sprinkling of fennel fronds keep the flavors light.

Preheat the oven to 400°F.

Arrange the fennel wedges in a single layer on a baking sheet, drizzle with the oil, and season with salt and pepper. Roast until the fennel is lightly browned and tender, about 12 minutes. Let cool.

Place a pizza stone in the oven and raise the oven temperature to 425°F.

Meanwhile, in a frying pan over medium-high heat, cook the sausage, breaking up the meat with a wooden spoon into marble-size pieces, until no pink remains, about 5 minutes. Transfer to a bowl to cool.

In a small bowl, stir together the ricotta, ½ teaspoon salt, and a few grinds of pepper.

On a lightly floured surface, roll out the dough to a 12-inch round. Transfer the dough to a floured pizza peel. Spread the ricotta mixture evenly over the dough, leaving a 1-inch border uncovered. Arrange the fennel wedges and sausage on top and sprinkle with the mozzarella.

Transfer the pizza to the preheated stone. Bake until the crust is crisp and golden brown, 7–8 minutes.

Using the pizza peel, transfer the pizza to a cutting board and garnish generously with fennel fronds. Cut the pizza into slices and serve.

Serves 4

1 fennel bulb, trimmed and cut into ¼-inch wedges, fronds reserved for garnish

3 tablespoons olive oil

Kosher salt and freshly ground pepper

6 oz mild Italian sausage, casings removed

½ cup ricotta cheese, drained

All-purpose flour, for dusting

1 ball (6 oz) Pizza Dough (pages 13–14)

½ cup (2 oz) shredded mozzarella cheese

Wild Mushroom Pizza with Thyme & Fontina

Use your favorite wild mushrooms in this elegant pizza, seeking out whatever is in season. Richly browned with butter and shallots, then finished with white wine and cream, the sautéed mushrooms are layered over a fontina-embellished white sauce to create a satisfying combination.

Place a pizza stone in the oven. Preheat the oven to 425°F.

In a large frying pan over medium heat, melt the butter. Add the shallot and cook, stirring occasionally, until softened, about 3 minutes. Add the mushrooms and cook, stirring occasionally, until beginning to caramelize, about 5 minutes. Add the garlic and cook, stirring occasionally, until fragrant, about 1 minute. Season with salt and pepper. Reduce the heat to medium-low, add the thyme sprigs and wine, and deglaze the pan, stirring to scrape up any browned bits from the bottom. Add the cream and cook, stirring constantly, until the liquid has evaporated, about 3 minutes. Let cool. Remove and discard the thyme sprigs.

On a lightly floured surface, roll out the dough to a 12-inch round. Transfer the dough to a floured pizza peel. Spread the white sauce evenly over the dough, leaving a 1-inch border uncovered. Sprinkle ½ cup of the cheese over the sauce. Spread the mushrooms evenly on top and sprinkle with the remaining ½ cup cheese.

Transfer the pizza to the preheated stone. Bake until the crust is crisp and golden brown, 7–8 minutes.

Using the pizza peel, transfer the pizza to a cutting board. Cut the pizza into slices and serve.

Serves 4

3 tablespoons unsalted butter

1 shallot, diced

6 oz mixed wild mushrooms, such as oyster, maitake, enoki, or beech, stemmed, brushed clean, and cut as needed into a uniform size

2 cloves garlic, minced

Kosher salt and freshly ground pepper

3 fresh thyme sprigs

2 tablespoons dry white wine

2 tablespoons heavy cream

All-purpose flour, for dusting

1 ball (6 oz) Pizza Dough (pages 13–14)

½ cup White Sauce (page 18)

1 cup (4 oz) shredded fontina cheese

Pizza with Kale, Pancetta & Chile Oil

Most lovers of Italian cuisine prefer kale and other hardy greens when they are slightly charred, which brings out the green's full, sweet flavor. This topping of kale, pancetta, and cheese is dense enough to hold up to a thick Sicilian crust (as here), but could also be divided between two rounds of thin crust instead.

Preheat the oven to 450°F.

In a frying pan over medium-high heat, cook the pancetta until crisp and cooked through, 7–10 minutes. Transfer to a paper towel–lined plate and let cool.

In a bowl, toss together the kale and olive oil, and season with salt and pepper.

Place the dough in a greased rimmed baking sheet and prepare as directed. Spread the white sauce evenly over the dough, leaving a 1-inch border uncovered. Arrange the pancetta and kale on top.

Bake until the crust is crisp and golden brown, 27–30 minutes.

Using the pizza peel, transfer the pizza to a cutting board, sprinkle with the cheese, and drizzle with chile oil. Cut the pizza into slices and serve.

Serves 8

¾ lb pancetta, cut into ¼-inch pieces

6 kale leaves, thick stems and ribs removed, leaves cut into ribbons

2 tablespoons olive oil

Kosher salt and freshly ground pepper

1 ball (14 oz) Sicilian Crust Dough (page 14)

1 cup White Sauce (page 18)

½ cup (2 oz) grated Parmesan cheese

Calabrian chile oil, for drizzling

Peach, Prosciutto & Arugula Pizza

Sweet peach, salty prosciutto, peppery arugula, and tangy balsamic make a dynamic quartet in this winning medley. To keep the arugula nice and crisp, scatter it over the pizza just before serving.

Place a pizza stone in the oven. Preheat the oven to 425°F.

On a lightly floured surface, roll out the dough to a 12-inch round. Transfer the dough to a floured pizza peel. Spread the pesto evenly over the dough, leaving a 1-inch border uncovered. Arrange the peach slices on top, season with salt and pepper, and drape the prosciutto among the peaches.

Transfer the pizza to the preheated stone. Bake until the crust is crisp and golden brown, 7–8 minutes.

Using the pizza peel, transfer the pizza to a cutting board, sprinkle with the cheese, drizzle with the balsamic glaze, and garnish with arugula. Cut the pizza into slices and serve.

Serves 4

All-purpose flour, for dusting

1 ball (6 oz) Pizza Dough (pages 13–14)

¼ cup Arugula Pesto (page 18)

1 cup sliced peaches

Kosher salt and freshly ground pepper

2 oz thinly sliced prosciutto

2 tablespoons (½ oz) grated Parmesan cheese

Balsamic glaze, for drizzling

Arugula leaves, for garnish

Add crushed red pepper flakes just before baking or offer them at the table for diners to add as desired.

Pizza with Broccolini, Sweet Onion & Feta

As with most brassicas, broccolini's wonderfully mellow, nutty taste is augmented by a quick charring in the oven. Mild sweet onion and feta cheese round out the toppings to create a pizza that's hearty enough for a thick crust or one made with cornmeal (page 13).

Place a pizza stone in the oven. Preheat the oven to 425°F.

In a bowl, toss together the broccolini, onion, and oil, and season with salt and black pepper.

On a lightly floured surface, roll out the dough to a 12-inch round. Transfer the dough to a floured pizza peel. Spread the tomato sauce evenly over the dough, leaving a 1-inch border uncovered. Arrange the broccolini and onion on top. Sprinkle with the feta, red pepper flakes, and 2 tablespoons of the Parmesan.

Transfer the pizza to the preheated stone. Bake until the crust is crisp and golden brown, 7–8 minutes.

Using the pizza peel, transfer the pizza to a cutting board and sprinkle with the remaining 2 tablespoons Parmesan. Cut the pizza into slices and serve.

Serves 4

4 oz broccolini, roughly chopped

¼ cup thinly sliced Vidalia or other sweet onion

1 tablespoon olive oil

Kosher salt and freshly ground black pepper

All-purpose flour, for dusting

1 ball (6 oz) Pizza Dough (pages 13–14)

⅓ cup Tomato Sauce (page 17)

⅓ cup crumbled feta cheese

1 teaspoon red pepper flakes

¼ cup (1 oz) grated Parmesan cheese

Meat Lover's Pizza

Topped with nuggets of Italian sausage, chunks of bacon, and sliced pepperoni, this pizza is a carnivore's dream. Add a garnish of sliced green onions plus red pepper flakes for a hit of heat right before serving, if you like.

Place a pizza stone in the oven. Preheat the oven to 425°F.

In a frying pan over medium-high heat, cook the sausage, breaking up the meat with a wooden spoon into marble-size pieces, until no pink remains, about 5 minutes. Transfer to a paper towel–lined plate to cool.

In the same pan over medium heat, cook the bacon, stirring occasionally, until just cooked through, about 5 minutes. Transfer to the paper towel–lined plate and set aside.

On a lightly floured surface, roll out the dough to a 12-inch round. Transfer the dough to a floured pizza peel. Spread the tomato sauce evenly over the dough, leaving a 1-inch border uncovered. Sprinkle with the cheese and arrange the sausage, bacon, and pepperoni on top.

Transfer the pizza to the preheated stone. Bake until the crust is crisp and golden brown, 7–8 minutes.

Using the pizza peel, transfer the pizza to a cutting board and sprinkle with the green onions and the red pepper flakes, if using. Cut the pizza into slices and serve.

Serves 4

3 oz Italian sausage, casings removed

¼ lb bacon, cut into 1-inch pieces

All-purpose flour, for dusting

1 ball (6 oz) Pizza Dough (pages 13–14)

½ cup Tomato Sauce (page 17)

¾ cup (3 oz) shredded mozzarella cheese

1 oz sliced pepperoni

2 green onions, thinly sliced on the diagonal

Red pepper flakes, for garnish (optional)

Barbecue Chicken Pizza with Salsa Verde

Cubes of white meat chicken and a fragrant barbecue sauce make a robust topping for pizza, while a bright salsa verde of green onions and cilantro lightens things up. To save time, swap in rotisserie chicken.

Fill a saucepan two-thirds full with water and bring to a boil over high heat. Reduce to a simmer, add the chicken, and cook until opaque and cooked through, about 20 minutes. Transfer the chicken to a cutting board and let cool, then cut into ½-inch cubes.

Meanwhile, place a pizza stone in the oven and preheat the oven to 425°F.

To make the salsa verde, in a food processor, combine the green onions, cilantro, red onion, and garlic and pulse until finely chopped. Add the oil and vinegar and process until incorporated, about 30 seconds. Season with salt and pepper.

Place the red onion in a bowl of ice water and let stand for 5 minutes, then drain and pat dry.

On a lightly floured surface, roll out the dough to a 12-inch round. Transfer the dough to a floured pizza peel. Spread the barbecue sauce evenly over the dough, leaving a 1-inch border uncovered. Arrange the chicken and red onion on top, season with salt and pepper, and sprinkle with the cheese.

Transfer the pizza to the preheated stone. Bake until the crust is crisp and golden brown, 7–8 minutes.

Using the pizza peel, transfer the pizza to a cutting board and drizzle all over with the salsa verde. Cut the pizza into slices and serve.

Serves 4

1 skinless, boneless chicken breast (about ½ lb)

FOR THE GREEN ONION SALSA VERDE

¼ cup chopped green onions

¼ cup fresh cilantro leaves

⅛ cup chopped red onion

1 small clove garlic

2 tablespoons olive oil

1 tablespoon red wine vinegar

Kosher salt and freshly ground pepper

⅓ red onion, thinly sliced

All-purpose flour, for dusting

1 ball (6 oz) Pizza Dough (pages 13–14)

⅓ cup barbecue sauce

Kosher salt and freshly ground pepper

½ cup (2 oz) shredded mozzarella cheese

Serrano Ham & Grilled Pineapple Pizza with Smoked Mozzarella

The classic Hawaiian-style pizza gets an update with serrano ham, smoked mozzarella cheese, and a shower of fresh cilantro leaves. Before topping the pizza, the pineapple slices are grilled to bring out their natural sweetness.

Place a pizza stone in the oven. Preheat the oven to 425°F.

Prepare a grill for direct-heat cooking over high heat, or preheat a grill pan on the stove top over high heat. Brush the grill rack or the pan with oil. Grill the pineapple slices, turning once, until nicely grill-marked, about 3 minutes on each side. Transfer to a plate and let cool.

On a lightly floured surface, roll out the dough to a 12-inch round. Transfer the dough to a floured pizza peel. Spread the tomato sauce evenly over the dough, leaving a 1-inch border uncovered. Arrange the pineapple slices on top, drape the serrano ham over the pineapple, and sprinkle with the cheese.

Transfer the pizza to the preheated stone. Bake until the crust is crisp and golden brown, 7–8 minutes.

Using the pizza peel, transfer the pizza to a cutting board and sprinkle with the cilantro. Cut the pizza into slices and serve.

Serves 4

Canola oil, for brushing

1½ cups sliced pineapple

All-purpose flour, for dusting

1 ball (6 oz) Pizza Dough (pages 13–14)

⅓ cup Tomato Sauce (page 17)

2 oz thinly sliced serrano ham

½ cup (2 oz) shredded smoked mozzarella cheese

¼ cup fresh cilantro leaves

Fresh basil is also a nice complement to the pineapple in this pizza, so use it instead of the cilantro if preferred.

In Italian kitchens, fresh fennel and lemon are classic complements to calamari.

Calamari Pizza with Shaved Fennel, Lemon & Spicy Aioli

As Italy is surrounded on three sides by coastline, pizzas featuring seafood caught in the local waters are popular in restaurants and home kitchens alike. Here, squid cooks to tender perfection in the high heat of the oven.

To make the spicy aioli, in a small bowl, stir together the mayonnaise, lemon juice, granulated garlic, and cayenne. Transfer to a small piping bag or a lock-top plastic bag and cut off the tip or a small corner. Set aside.

In a small bowl, toss together the shaved fennel and 1 tablespoon of the oil, and season with salt and black pepper. In another small bowl, toss together the squid and the remaining 1 tablespoon oil, and season lightly with salt and black pepper.

On a lightly floured surface, roll out the dough to a 10-inch round. Transfer the dough to a floured pizza peel. Spread the white sauce evenly over the dough, leaving a 1-inch border uncovered. Arrange the shaved fennel and lemon slices on top, followed by the squid.

Transfer the pizza to the preheated stone. Bake until the crust is crisp and golden brown, 7–8 minutes.

Using the pizza peel, transfer the pizza to a cutting board, drizzle with the spicy aioli, garnish with fennel fronds, and sprinkle with red pepper flakes, if using. Cut the pizza into slices and serve.

Serves 4

FOR THE SPICY AIOLI

2 tablespoons mayonnaise

1 teaspoon fresh lemon juice

½ teaspoon granulated garlic

¼ teaspoon cayenne pepper

½ fennel bulb, trimmed and thinly shaved, fronds reserved for garnish

2 tablespoons olive oil

Kosher salt and freshly ground black pepper

3 oz squid rings and tentacles, rinsed and patted dry

All-purpose flour, for dusting

1 ball (6 oz) Pizza Dough (pages 13–14)

½ cup White Sauce (page 18)

½ lemon, very thinly sliced, seeds removed

Red pepper flakes, for garnish (optional)

Salsiccia Pizza with Padrón Peppers

In this twist on the popular sausage-topped pizza, sweet spring onion and earthy Padrón peppers make a great match for the meat. Be forewarned: Although most of these peppers are mild, the occasional one will pack some heat. If Padróns are unavailable, swap in half of a thinly sliced jalapeño chile.

Place a pizza stone in the oven. Preheat the oven to 425°F.

In a frying pan over medium-high heat, cook the sausage, breaking up the meat with a wooden spoon into marble-size pieces, until no pink remains, about 5 minutes. Transfer to a bowl to cool.

In a bowl, toss together the Padrón peppers and oil, and season with salt and pepper.

On a lightly floured surface, roll out the dough into a 14-inch oval. Transfer the dough to a floured pizza peel. Sprinkle the cheese evenly around the perimeter of the dough oval, leaving a 1-inch border uncovered. Fold the dough edge over the cheese and press firmly to enclose. Spread the tomato sauce evenly over the dough, leaving the cheese-stuffed rim uncovered. Arrange the sausage and onion slices on top, followed by the Padrón peppers.

Transfer the pizza to the preheated stone. Bake until the crust is crisp and golden brown, 7–8 minutes.

Using the pizza peel, transfer the pizza to a cutting board and sprinkle with the cheese. Cut the pizza into slices and serve.

Serves 4

6 oz Italian sausage, casings removed

1/3 cup Padrón peppers

1 tablespoon olive oil

Kosher salt and freshly ground pepper

All-purpose flour, for dusting

1 ball (6 oz) Pizza Dough (pages 13–14)

1½ cups (6 oz) shredded mozzarella cheese

1/3 cup Tomato Sauce (page 17)

1 spring onion or 4 green onions, white and pale green parts, thinly sliced

1/4 cup (1 oz) grated pecorino cheese

A mozzarella-stuffed crust is an unexpected embellisment to this robust pie. If you prefer a plain one, simply omit the cheese

Pepperoni Pizza with Shaved Red Onion, Castelvetrano Olives & Honey

The much-loved pepperoni pizza gets a makeover, sharing the spotlight with red onion and meaty Castelvetrano olives. Honey may seem like an unusual addition to this savory pie, but the last-minute drizzle helps meld the ingredients into perfect harmony.

Place a pizza stone in the oven. Preheat the oven to 425°F.

On a lightly floured surface, roll out the dough to a 12-inch round. Transfer the dough to a floured pizza peel. Spread the oil evenly over the dough, leaving a 1-inch border uncovered. Arrange the olives, onion, and pepperoni on top and sprinkle with 2 tablespoons of the cheese.

Transfer the pizza to the preheated stone. Bake until the crust is crisp and golden brown, 7–8 minutes.

Using the pizza peel, transfer the pizza to a cutting board, drizzle with the honey, and sprinkle with the remaining 2 tablespoons cheese. Cut the pizza into slices and serve.

Serves 4

All-purpose flour, for dusting

1 ball (6 oz) Pizza Dough (pages 13–14)

1 tablespoon olive oil

½ cup pitted Castelvetrano or other green olives, halved

⅓ cup thinly sliced red onion

2 oz sliced pepperoni

¼ cup (1 oz) grated Parmesan cheese

2 tablespoons honey

Ham & Asparagus Pizza with Caramelized Onions & Fried Egg

A few minutes in a hot oven is all that's needed to transform thin strips of asparagus into a tender topping for pizza. For easy prep, shave the spears with a serrated vegetable peeler that's designed for soft-skinned fruits and vegetables. A runny fried egg makes this pie suitable for any time of day.

In a frying pan over low heat, melt the butter. Add the onion and season with salt and pepper. Cook, stirring occasionally, until the onion is meltingly tender and rich brown in color, about 40 minutes; do not let it burn. Let cool.

Meanwhile, place a pizza stone in the oven and preheat the oven to 425°F.

In a bowl, toss together the asparagus and the 2 teaspoons oil, and season with salt and pepper.

On a lightly floured surface, roll out the dough to a 12-inch round. Transfer the dough to a floured pizza peel. Arrange the cheese evenly over the dough, leaving a 1-inch border uncovered. Top with the caramelized onion and ham, followed by the asparagus.

Transfer the pizza to the preheated stone. Bake until the crust is crisp and golden brown, 7–8 minutes.

Meanwhile, in a small nonstick frying pan over medium-low heat, warm the 1 tablespoon oil. Crack the egg into the pan and cook until the white is set but the yolk is still runny, about 3 minutes.

Using the pizza peel, transfer the pizza to a cutting board and top with the fried egg. Cut the pizza into slices and serve.

Serves 4

3 tablespoons unsalted butter

1 small yellow onion, thinly sliced

Kosher salt and freshly ground pepper

4 asparagus spears, trimmed and thinly shaved lengthwise

2 teaspoons plus 1 tablespoon olive oil

All-purpose flour, for dusting

1 ball (6 oz) Pizza Dough (pages 13–14)

4 slices (about 3 oz) provolone cheese

2 oz thinly sliced country ham

1 large egg

Dried oregano, fresh garlic, and
good-quality olive oil are key
ingredients to have on hand
when making pizza at home.

Index

A
Anchovy & Artichoke Pizza, 37
Artichokes
 Artichoke & Anchovy Pizza, 37
 Quattro Staggioni Pizza, 25
Arugula
 Arugula Pesto, 18
 Mozzarella & Grana Padano Pizza with Truffle Oil & Arugula, 31
 Peach, Prosciutto & Arugula Pizza, 46
Asparagus
 Ham & Asparagus Pizza with Caramelized Onions & Fried Egg, 59
 Pizza with Shaved Asparagus, Melted Leeks & Burrata, 22

B
Bacon
 Meat Lover's Pizza, 50
 Pizza with Kale, Pancetta & Chile Oil, 45
 Potato, Bacon & Rosemary Pizza, 26
Barbecue Chicken Pizza with Salsa Verde, 51
Basil
 Basil Pesto, 18
 Heirloom Tomato Pizza Margherita, 36
 Pesto Pizza with Summer Squash, Sweet Corn & Pecorino, 35
Broccolini, Sweet Onion & Feta, Pizza with, 49

C
Calamari Pizza with Shaved Fennel, Lemon & Spicy Aioli, 55
Cheese
 Chorizo & Manchego Pizza with Oregano Oil, 40
 Fig & Prosciutto Pizza with Caramelized Onions & Gorgonzola, 39
 Heirloom Tomato Pizza Margherita, 36
 Mozzarella & Grana Padano Pizza with Truffle Oil & Arugula, 31
 Pesto Pizza with Summer Squash, Sweet Corn & Pecorino, 35
 Pizza with Broccolini, Sweet Onion & Feta, 49
 Pizza with Shaved Asparagus, Melted Leeks & Burrata, 22
 Sausage Pizza with Fennel & Ricotta, 42
 Sei Formaggi Pizza, 32
 Serrano Ham & Grilled Pineapple Pizza with Smoked Mozzarella, 52
 Wild Mushroom Pizza with Thyme & Fontina, 43
Chicken, Barbecue, Pizza with Salsa Verde, 51
Chorizo & Manchego Pizza with Oregano Oil, 40
Corn, Sweet, Summer Squash & Pecorino, Pesto Pizza with, 35
Cornmeal Pizza Dough, 13

E
Egg, Fried, & Caramelized Onions, Ham & Asparagus Pizza with, 59
Equipment, 8

F
Fennel
 Calamari Pizza with Shaved Fennel, Lemon & Spicy Aioli, 55
 Sausage Pizza with Fennel & Ricotta, 42
Fig & Prosciutto Pizza with Caramelized Onions & Gorgonzola, 39

G
Gluten-Free Pizza Dough, 14
Guanciale & Fried Sage Leaves, Pizza with, 28

H
Ham
 Fig & Prosciutto Pizza with Caramelized Onions & Gorgonzola, 39
 Ham & Asparagus Pizza with Caramelized Onions & Fried Egg, 59
 Peach, Prosciutto & Arugula Pizza, 46
 Quattro Staggioni Pizza, 25
 Serrano Ham & Grilled Pineapple Pizza with Smoked Mozzarella, 52
Heirloom Tomato Pizza Margherita, 36

K

Kale, Pancetta & Chile Oil, Pizza with, 45

L

Leeks, Melted, Shaved Asparagus & Burrata, Pizza with, 22

M

Meat Lover's Pizza, 50
Mozzarella & Grana Padano Pizza with Truffle Oil & Arugula, 31
Mushrooms
    Quattro Staggioni Pizza, 25
    Wild Mushroom Pizza with Thyme & Fontina, 43

O

Olives
    Artichoke & Anchovy Pizza, 37
    Pepperoni Pizza with Shaved Red Onion, Castelvetrano Olives & Honey, 58
    Quattro Staggioni Pizza, 25
Onions
    Fig & Prosciutto Pizza with Caramelized Onions & Gorgonzola, 39
    Ham & Asparagus Pizza with Caramelized Onions & Fried Egg, 59
    Pepperoni Pizza with Shaved Red Onion, Castelvetrano Olives & Honey, 58
    Pizza with Broccolini, Sweet Onion & Feta, 49

P

Peach, Prosciutto & Arugula Pizza, 46

Pepperoni Pizza with Shaved Red Onion, Castelvetrano Olives & Honey, 58
Peppers
    Romesco Sauce, 17
    Salsiccia Pizza with Padrón Peppers, 56
Pesto
    Arugula Pesto, 18
    Basil Pesto, 18
    Pesto Pizza with Summer Squash, Sweet Corn & Pecorino, 35
Pineapple, Grilled, & Serrano Ham Pizza with Smoked Mozzarella, 52
Pizza dough
    about, 10–11
    Cornmeal Pizza Dough, 13
    Gluten-Free Pizza Dough, 14
    Regular Crust Slow Dough, 13
    Sicilian Crust Dough, 14
    Thin Crust Fast Dough, 13
Pork. See Bacon; Guanciale; Ham; Sausages
Potato, Bacon & Rosemary Pizza, 26

Q

Quattro Staggioni Pizza, 25

R

Regular Crust Slow Dough, 13
Romesco Sauce, 17

S

Salsa Verde, Barbecue Chicken Pizza with, 51
Salsiccia Pizza with Padrón Peppers, 56
Sauces
    Arugula Pesto, 18
    Basil Pesto, 18

Romesco Sauce, 17
Tomato Sauce, 17
White Sauce, 18
Sausages
    Chorizo & Manchego Pizza with Oregano Oil, 40
    Meat Lover's Pizza, 50
    Salsiccia Pizza with Padrón Peppers, 56
    Sausage Pizza with Fennel & Ricotta, 42
Seafood
    Artichoke & Anchovy Pizza, 37
    Calamari Pizza with Shaved Fennel, Lemon & Spicy Aioli, 55
    White Pizza with Fresh Clams & Tarragon, 29
Sei Formaggi Pizza, 32
Serrano Ham & Grilled Pineapple Pizza with Smoked Mozzarella, 52
Sicilian Crust Dough, 14
Squash, Summer, Sweet Corn & Pecorino, Pesto Pizza with, 35

T

Thin Crust Fast Dough, 13
Tomatoes
    Heirloom Tomato Pizza Margherita, 36
    Tomato Sauce, 17
Toppings, about, 21

W

White Pizza with Fresh Clams & Tarragon, 29
White Sauce, 18
Wild Mushroom Pizza with Thyme & Fontina, 43

Use plenty of flour on the
work surface, rolling pin,
and pizza peel to prevent
the dough from sticking.

The Pizza Cookbook

Conceived and produced by Weldon Owen
in collaboration with Williams Sonoma, Inc.
3250 Van Ness Avenue, San Francisco, CA 94109

Printed in Turkey
First printed in 2018
10 9 8 7 6 5 4

Library of Congress
Cataloging-in-Publication
data is available.

ISBN 13: 978-1-68188-466-0

Weldon Owen International
1045 Sansome Street, Suite 100
San Francisco, CA 94111
www.weldonowen.com

President & Publisher Roger Shaw
SVP, Sales & Marketing Amy Kaneko
Associate Publisher Amy Marr
Senior Editor Lisa Atwood
Creative Director Kelly Booth
Art Director Marisa Kwek
Designer Meghan Hildebrand
Production Director Michelle Duggan
Imaging Manager Don Hill

Photographer Erin Scott
Food Stylist Lillian Kang
Prop Stylist Kerrie Sherrell Walsh

ACKNOWLEDGMENTS

Weldon Owen wishes to thank the following people for their generous support in producing this book: Kris Balloun, Barbara Brenner, Lou Bustamante, Josephine Hsu, Marisa Kwek, Rachel Markowitz, Alexis Mersel, Nicola Parisi, Elizabeth Parson, Emerson Tenney, and Andrea Trezza.